Everything reaches out to everything else

New Women's Voices Series, No. 155

poems by

Jacqueline De Angelis

Finishing Line Press
Georgetown, Kentucky

Everything reaches out to everything else

New Women's Voices Series, No. 155

Copyright © 2020 by Jacqueline De Angelis
ISBN 978-1-64662-332-7 First Edition
All rights reserved under International and Pan-American Copyright Conventions. No part of this book may be reproduced in any manner whatsoever without written permission from the publisher, except in the case of brief quotations embodied in critical articles and reviews.

ACKNOWLEDGMENTS

Thanks to the editors of the magazines and anthologies in which these poems first appeared.

"Things no one knows" and "Siamese" *Agni* 46, 1997.
"That dog" *Emily Dickinson Award Anthology*, 1997.
"Atwater" *International Quarterly*, 1997.
"Atwater" *Another City: Writing from Los Angeles*, David Ulin, City Lights Press, 2001.
"Under the Valencia tree invisible to Moselle's family celebration" *Minute Magazine* issue 7 and *Minute Magazine Podcast*, 2019.

There are so many to thank for their mentoring, but this group influenced me the most over time: Eloise Klein Healy, Anne Winters, Liam Rector, and David Lehman.

For many years I have benefited considerably from working with other writers but most particularly from the unflinching criticism and encouragement of Noelle Sickels and Julia Mary Gibson.

I am always grateful to Ricardo for our days of togetherness.

Publisher: Leah Huete de Maines
Editor: Christen Kincaid
Cover Art: Ricardo Medina
Author Photo: Ricardo Medina
Cover Design: Elizabeth Maines McCleavy

Order online: www.finishinglinepress.com
also available on amazon.com

Author inquiries and mail orders:
Finishing Line Press
P. O. Box 1626
Georgetown, Kentucky 40324
U. S. A.

Table of Contents

Things no one knows 1

Madera Avenue 3

That dog 4

Siamese 5

At Sav-On 6

Atwater 8

Under the Valencia tree invisible to Moselle's family
   celebration 21

Math 22

Under circumstances 23

Everything reaches out to everything else 25

One 28

*To my cousin, Polly,
for giving me the love of words and reading.*

Things no one knows

The evil eye is on me.
Take a look at the plumbing, how the water in the tub (cold water) started to slow down.
I ignore many things.
One must or else collapse.
It got down to a trickle.
There is evil.
Eventually I call.
Jesse won't take new clients but I'm in his book.
He'll come on Friday.
Friday he can't come because of a house that has no water.
I am not an emergency.
Monday at 3pm he taps a few pipes.
It works, he says, but not for long.
Nothing works for long but in this case not for long is right around the corner.
Things happen on holidays and there is no one around to help you.
The pipes are no good from the house to the street.
Look at the plaster in the bedroom corner by the dirty clothes basket.
The patch I patched with spackle fell off.
No earthquakes, no leaks, it fell out of nowhere onto my black rayon dress.
Now there is a scab on the ceiling.
Can't see the face of Jesus.
No Virgin Mary silhouette.
A sick continent surrounded by a gray sea.
Look, the track lights in the kitchen.
On.
Then.
Won't go on.
Then on again.
See the garbage disposal and the half mashed up shrimp egg rolls I fished up.
Need a new one, says Jesse who will come Thursday but arrives on Tuesday.

Where's the short?
I tell Ali I noticed it when the radio would go off and on.
Now the door locks do the same.
Now I can't see the speedometer or the time.
Now the battery is drained and no jump starts it.

How else would you explain it?
Life is full of messages interrupted.
Calls for garlic in the bra.
Just a clove.
Keep it private.
A sweet variety works best.
Of course there are smelling salts.
A small bottle on an altar.
Some dabbed on the wrist.
Sends the evil back to the one who set it in motion.
The front screen door won't lock or locks and won't open from the outside.
Same is true for the toaster oven.
Snap knob in my hand.
Then the couch, rip along the seam, yellow cotton stuffing is a kitten toy.
I head for the electric sweeper.
Back away and grab the broom and dust pan.
The Turkish refrigerator starts to leak.
It freezes and then what's frozen melts and settles in the vegetable bin.
What's in the vegetable bin turns to slime.
If you look over anyone's life you'll find reasons.
The intentional discourtesy.
The misstatements.
The times I've cut in to get ahead on the 5 freeway interchange from the 110.
The rear-view mirror, what's it doing in my hand?

Madera Avenue

I want revelations
on a night like this.

Fall wind with watery
flavor, little Sandy
rubs her spice on sidewalks,
Norm and Georgine
bludgeon the walls
of their remodel,
guys across the street come out front
to stare at their privacy planting,
someone drives by despite
obvious car trouble.

I need something profound
not just pluck
fruit off the ground,
weed weed weed,
send in pests to
remove pests.

Southern Pacific freight train
blasts through intersections,
incessant river frogs croak, two
gun shots at the river.

Notary next door
calls in his basketball kid
bounce, bounce and rim.

Looking down a
spider-threaded
vermilion
bougainvillea petal
twirls, pauses,
twists,
twirls again
mechanical.

That dog

Nowhere to park tonight, the young red dog in the street is on the loose.
Unclipped ears and shiny coat it looks for the softhearted.
I stumble to the front and stare, red young dog in the street.
It wants me to open the gate but I stubbed my toe on broken concrete.

Unclipped ears and shiny coat he looks for the softhearted.
The entire world's gone sour. I feel only one thing.
It wants me to open the gate but I stubbed my toe on broken concrete.
I smell ham; someone had ham. Pineapple slice tooth-picked to maple glazed skin.

The entire world's gone sour. I feel my toe.
Someone had fish for dinner, fried with the whiskers on, eyes white.
I smell ham; someone had ham. Pineapple slice tooth-picked to maple gazed skin.
I ate Thai takeout: green curry, sweet ribs, black mushrooms with greens.

Someone had fish, fried with the whiskers on, eyes white.
I am not going to rescue a dog. The neediness in every gesture. (Repelling!)
I ate leftover Thai takeout: green curry, sweet ribs, black mushrooms with greens.
I am watching a red dog study the street (what goes on in such a mind?).

I am not going to rescue the dog. The repelling neediness in every gesture.
His paw print on my muddy sidewalk, he sticks his sniffing nose through chain link.
I am watching a red dog (what goes on in such a mind?).
You can't come in. Go away, I say.
His paw print on my muddy sidewalk, there is no way I'm taking in a dog, he sticks his sniffing nose through chain link.

Siamese

At the moment you see them slit open like chickens,
you are lacing your right shoe. Twins joined are separated on Channel
7 News.

One has more of the heart but their livers will split perfectly.

This could do damage. See those organs respond to the knife.
It's never easy staring straight into the contents. The melody

follows you everywhere; repulsive as pupas on public TV.

You are not like this.
Man never walked on the moon.

If this is to show you how marvelous we are it doesn't do the trick.
You're caught in a cheap magic show, saw serrating belly skin.

You can't get past the slimy screws and muscles—what is body?

The news moves on and who wouldn't be relieved. Recently war is all in the air; bloodless logistics that reassure. Your feet secure, you walk out on the lawn,

the day grays, fan palms don't flutter. A truck full of stillness, the street has no moon.

At Sav-On

How
in the middle
of the night
it feels
to be standing
at a counter
across
from someone who
every single night
sells
what someone
desperately
needs when
the rest of us
are asleep.
Here under
extraordinary
circumstances
I would
be sleeping
normally am
and any nightly
transactions made
are
with shadowy stand-ins
of myself;
but here the bottle has
my name on it,
round gels
inside will
curb hacking
so, stepping
out of
automatic doors
into
the sweep of

parking spaces
toward my
suddenly shrunken
car
the night ness
of a night
like this
is stunning.
Street lights on Riverside
are brackish,
Southern Pacific
cranks through
our splendid
sagging neighborhoods.
Day
is just
too bright,
since when
was it
that
I noticed
Orion alone
over
a backlit
bare branched
dark?

Atwater

I
If I am on the river, if I am staring in the water, if I see all the plastic cups, a whiffle ball, sharp objects swiftly moving, miscellaneous wrappers, no buttons,

then, where do I enter?

II
You can walk
under bridges, through one city

and then another without noticing. Look, a drowning shopping cart. In it a list:
toothpaste,
candles,
juice,
pink dishwashing soap.

III
The water isn't potable. It doesn't irrigate. It will not serve us.
The river is passing.

IV
This river is no river of the future.

V
There is a boy with black hair. His father passes the kite string.
The boy looks up. The kite is yellow and probably black. Certainly dark in spots. A bee maybe? The string slips. The boy doesn't want.

The kite is going one way, the river another.

VI
Rain runoff rushes down Arroyo Calabasas, Bell Creek, San Gabriel mountain canyons, Compton creek. It mixes with our gray water. If we are unlucky the sewers run into it.

Terminates not at Playa del Rey, King of Pacific beaches, but a container port where sound diminishes water.

VII
We are wry about it.
We do not sit and reminisce about the night we rode this river, self-sufficient, the moon glimmering in waves.

We do not yearn for the slap of river on shore.

It is us this river. We slough off. We ride over back and forth and over and over and do not call its name. We do not turn in the dark to spell it on the broad back of a lover.

We have an ocean. But that is another story.

VIII
The Mississippi is commerce. The Mahoning is canoeing clubs. Seine sublime. Ganges, religious. In the Amazon swim fish that can bite OFF your feet. Now look at how movies have made rivers so frightening they appear in my dreams.

IX
Why are you surprised; it is a river therefore people drown.
They watch too much TV and consequently have no experience.
The swift deep is something they learn too late.

We don't stand, stare,
throw coins,
think of it as travel,
salvation,
escape.

X
People have jumped. From the spanning bridges. Off the viaducts.
They heard the laugh concrete has.
I don't actually remember the story of the woman who leapt from the bridge with her baby.
I heard it. I saw the daughter in Thursday's paper. The details are hazy.
I remember the part where it said she was lonely. That struck me.

Who isn't really?

XI
I live on the river bank. Not the current but the natural shore.
Some hot nights the river smells. Damp clothes left in a plastic bag.
Some sort of excremental mold. Something the cat dragged in.

I do not stand and stare. I do not whisper its name to the broad back of my lover.
If this is a river…

XII
The daughter, all grown sitting at her kitchen table, said, in the Life & Times section, that she forgave her mother. "My mother was just lonely." We can all understand that.
This forgiving daughter with unkempt hair fascinates me. See her in the shabby four-color of newspapers. The printer's rosette off-register; she is cyan, yellow, black, redder than dreams.

XIII
We are wry about her mother at dinner. Wire monkey mother. Mother that dresses you up
to jump off a bridge.

XIV
If this is a river it has no dreams.

XV

No, it has one dream.

XVI
Where do I enter?

XVII
When you live this near you have frogs and June bugs. If you lived one street further you would have the June bugs but not the frogs. You would not hear the cars on the Golden State freeway, either.

Some years the June bugs stay until July. The frogs less regular.
You have more in your yard if you have a dog and not a cat.
If you go down to the river at night you can hear frogs in the stream of vehicles.

You would not want to go down to the river at night. Remember, this isn't a river of dreams, you do not toss coins for wishes, there is no salvation at this shore, no one whispers its name into your ear.

XVIII
Here is the historia of el Rio.
Listen. This is before the Spanish altered the world.

"Some of the old men were smoking pipes well made of baked clay and they puffed at us three mouthfuls of smoke. We gave them a little tobacco and glass beads, and they went away well pleased. . . After crossing the river we entered a large vineyard of wild grapes and an infinity of rosebushes in full bloom. . .After traveling about half a league we came to the village of this region, the people of which on seeing us, came out into the road. As they drew near they began to howl like wolves; they greeted us and wished to give us seeds, but we did not accept them. Seeing this, they threw some handfuls of them on the ground and the rest in the air. (Bolton 1927:147)."

XIX
The neighborhood ice cream truck plays "Fascination."
In the winds, in the blasting heat, right through the fall, it is the background. Fascination.
I stop. Look around my garden. Notice what I can.

It never fails, I sing a line, I do not know the real words to this song.

The freight trains follow the river like a fascination.

The Golden State freeway follows the river like a snake. No, that's not it. The freeway
hems the river. That's not it . . . .

The wild grasses break through the concrete channel and grow promiscuous. They regreen her in clumps.

The foreign reeds grow straight down her spine.

XX
The river goes one way, people another.

My neighbor Moselle never liked the smell of this river.

When Moselle first laid eyes on it—it was when people took pride—
it was when you could trust what was in the water and who came to
your front door.
She couldn't speak for anyone else.

It smelled like an infinity of roses.

XXI
Floribunda I am promised at the Home Depot nursery.

"Blaze
Masses of bright-red 3" blooms cover this
popular climber spring through fall.
Strong canes reaching… display a profusion of eye-
catching, brilliant color…

Water thoroughly, weekly."

Plant it at the corner of the house and it will climb like the climbing
roses of Spain.

My mother says, you'll be sorry. My mother sees it attack the roof tiles.
My father the plumbing. I am going to see an infinity of roses.

XXII
This river is paying for its past anarchy. It is restricted, under
observation; police copters, news choppers, Stealth bomber on the way
to Dodger Stadium.

They scan for floating bodies.

How can anyone decipher the homeless river life under the Los Feliz bridge?

We who live here do so at our own peril. We who live on the shore ignore much. We can hear the river.

We live with gun shots, mortgages, gangs, landlords, out of old Winnebagos parked riverside.

They never tell you a thing about this channel when you live here.

It's a channel, isn't it? It isn't a river, is it?

XXIII

"We forded the Rio ... which descends with great rapidity from the canyon through which it leaves the mountains and enters the plains. All the country that we saw on this day's march appeared to us most suitable for the production of all kinds of grain and fruit."(Teggart 1911:181).

Batata,
maize,
tomatl,
ahuacatl (ah'-wah-cah-tl),
chicle,
cacauatl (kah-kah'-wah-tl)
papas.

"When early British golfers were playing with a ball made of feathers packed into a leather cover, Indians were playing a game with a ball made of rubber." (Teggart 1911:181)... they began to howl like wolves; they greeted us and wished to give us seeds, but we did not accept them

(Bolton 1927:147)...."

XXIV
Coming home. Stuck in traffic. All of us resigned but cunning.
On the viaduct, over the river, we do not move, it moves.
Here transportation is a toy; speed's a memory. All our achievements fallow misrepresentations. We've missed the mark somehow.
We've missed appointments, births, love. Fathers walk away. Dinners cool; down on our luck, death in the air, we are struck with the smell of rotting dog.

What if the river is liquid god?

I can't get that mother out of my mind.
I bring her up at lunch. Boss asks, Who do you think you are?
Singular, lonely, had enough fiction for one life.
I laugh, the arugula leaves, alligators at the tip of my fork, flap.

XXV
I am the jumping woman. I think of diving all the time. Let me out of this car...
The water is fine... An infinity of roses,... seeds flung in the air.

We know this. We ALL know the KNOCK in our ear.

If god is a liquid, if this is a river...

XXVI
There is nothing you can be told that you don't already know.
Don't ask a river.
Don't run your firm hand along its slippery thigh.
Don't spill your drunk guts out, pat your belly and think

you gave yourself to it, fed your real self to this deep slim channel.
Hollow, hollow your friends yawn on the shore. There is nothing
I can tell you that you don't already know.

XXVII
chan.nel (chan'el) n. Abbr. chan.1. The bed of a stream or river.2. The
deeper part of a river or harbor, especially a deep navigable passage.3.
A trench, furrow, or groove.4.. Electronics. A specified frequency
band for the transmission and reception of electromagnetic signals,
as for television signals. 5. The medium through which a spirit guide
purportedly communicates with the physical world.

XXVIII
Sit and look at it, go ahead, come on, hurry up, scoot, pick it up,
go on go.

Sit on slanted concrete. Watch water. Look, eddies. See the pied-billed
grebe dive rather than fly. Ignore the traffic. Over there, the great
cosmopolitan egret—nuptial plumage—stands, reflects in the current.
Sit, sit by the river and want.

XXIX
Clean the air and your own heart.
Drink all the bottled water you can.
Drink it all day long if need be.
Look, we are water. Our veins: what are they but a personal river?

Do you stare at water and think of your affinities? Have you ever?
When you see it (hostage) follow a cement course, what do you see?

XXX
You can walk under bridges, through one city without noticing

you are in another.

Where is our empathy?

Life shouldn't be so hard. All we want is to be liked, admired if possible, just not hated.

But, we do not leave well enough alone. We do not let things set. We do not give things peace.

XXXI
The mother who leapt, got up and got dressed then dressed the baby.

The mother broke. The baby daughter bounced.
Was it notoriety she wanted them to land in?
Was it more of the same? The ordinary list?
Toothpaste,
dishwashing soap,
pink juice.

At the sink scrubbing pans the cinematic me
jumps off buildings, drives cars into walls, off the edge of cliffs.
I am lonely, the dishwater is tepid.
I don't have the energy to cleanser the sink so
I jump, crash, drown Very dramatic.

So's the funeral.
Fewer people come than in the past. I've grown more realistic.
But they still regret my cold body laid out.
They should have called me more.
They might have had me over for a little something once in awhile.

Have I told you about this pain I have? I've been talking about it for years but no one listens.
I've gone from one thing to the next and it never leaves me. The number

of things I've tried, the amount of money I've thrown at it. The time it
has eaten away.
Legion, all of it.

And what good does it do to tell you about it!

XXXII
Had enough fiction for one life?

XXXIII
Let me gather my heart and lock it. A raven settles
in the apricot tree. All green, all hard, all raven waver.

There are so many ways to be famous but to be happy you must trust
the small.

XXXIV
What do you know of loneliness?

Don't turn away.
Without quizzes
without note pads
with all of the years brushed away;
think.

Don't turn to me,

XXXV
Here is where I enter, proctor
in these cold times brought by various product lines.
Elicits desired response.
I fail myself in check-out lines.

Always out of something.

XXXVI
Here is where I am a part of the whole,
a part of the problem, and I can't make myself stop
the purchase. Home late from work
I can't deal with recycling plastic and one slips to the trash.

If this river is liquid god, What have I done?

This morning I stood on the porch staring.
Should I paint it again or tile it once and for all?
Is it a bad entrance?

Anything happens when truth is not the point.

XXXVII
There is no prayer wheel turning over the rush of water; this isn't Tibet.
The ancestors are not burned at the shore, this isn't India.
No gold in pan, there's no Rush. No fish spawn.
No bend in this river that isn't planned.
No gift of seeds.
No roses, no, not anymore.

Because we can.
Because we can
Human's nasty eye and moneyed hand.

We are in a lot of trouble but carpe diem, don't worry we do not live that long.

XXXVIII
Deal the cards, as we say in my family when somebody talks too long.

Here I stand at the gritty brink of this river with my particular set of genes in hand.

Deal the cards.

Under the Valencia tree invisible to Moselle's family celebration

I know what it means to be in a generational kitchen, the whirl of open wounds, variety of snacks; all bound by repetition of cells and habit.

The night absorbs 10 o'clock news, melody, some hammering. This is summer, which explains everything: tomatoes blush, plums drop into palms, hard pears shape into women who could spur the dogs.

The pale city world is curbside for young men, brown
Beer bottles cool in hand, their intermittent roars fill the long envelope of night as if wild roses still bud from this wasted terrain.

Wind juggles the oranges above me, the evening passenger train (soundtrack of longing) runs the length of scars, bound north. Moselle's family folds in, each to their familiar bed, each to hear another's dreams.

Math

He thinks I am generous most of the time
but not at the short-hole golf coffee shop, so he adds to the tip I leave.

This isn't about waiters.

Babe, what about those busboys?

I look over at them, moving in and out of the kitchen, around the inside tables, then the outside table with the faded metal striped umbrella where we always sit.

He just wants to know one thing from me. Babe, what do you think they get paid?

He pays at the register. I wait in the parking lot, watch the golfers tee off.

Walking through the lot to his 63 Chevy step-side pickup, he adds nothing to the super-sized cup of the beggar.

When he starts the pickup, the straight six L250 growls.
Hey, I left over 20% for the tip and that's more than the chart recommended.

Yeah, no problem, he says—a chart, it's just so American.

On the way home I open the wind-wing, catch moist air as we drive past Griffith Park over Hyperion bridge where the LA river low rides to Long Beach.

Babe, you don't realize how that extra dollar makes their day.

Under circumstances

I have gone mad. Clearly. Deeply. There are no controls to this. No head room. But there are fans and snoring dogs.

How many sanitizing washes are in the life of a dishwashing machine?

When met with disorder. Met with relentlessness. When both join up and a kitchen rodent is involved, reason, judgement, sacredness turns and leaves the house.

No, I take that back, common sense is thrown out with the bath towel and the pasta roller.

I don't say this out loud but I say innumerable times, why is this happening to me?

I've left out of this confessional the pox I put on someone else's house.

A politician. You wouldn't think, in this case, the pox would boomerang.

And this is how far I've landed from the obvious. A rainy winter after a 5-year drought. A faulty cat door (no cat lives here now, another story) and an apparent ingress.

I don't co-exist with this species. I am not a turd-in-my-silverware-drawer kind of human. I don't forgive tiny bite marks in heirloom multi-colored plum tomatoes.

Madness is individual. Dripping water does not seem torture. I've had a native black tarantula fall on to my head without becoming prey to tarantism.

This is where frantic, frenzied, ferocious has the makings of tattoo. Where the live trap solicits a tee-hee, haw-haw, cackle. Where I stalk the reaper and the answer is me.

Many times, I have had a hummingbird fly in. Sample several rooms, go all the way to the apex. Gentle, unflappable, composed.

I assist, waving a red dish towel beyond the open door.

Everything reaches out to everything else

Here is the world I live in,
my circle of light.
Streets mapped lead

to impassable trails;
trespassers snidely
remind me
that no one owns
anything, really.
And I get this is truth
but only
in the abstract.

The flawless advertisement follows
me from screen to
screen.
Is this what
togetherness means
in a world without
collective desire,
where everything curls
toward the blue light
of merchandise?

I woke up alive again and put on my shoes
even though I couldn't find my purse.
I go about my business
even if it isn't actually business,
even if it is no more
than wash things,
sweep,
try my hand at
pickles or cheese.
While all the while my
chattering brain spews loose

paragraphs I don't
want others
to hear, and if they did, how
would they address me?

In the moonlight beach
sand looks clean
but is pale trash,
in the neighborhood cars
hit and run,
in the evening, parks are
sprayed
and sprayed again.

In the mornings
little ones
come to dig their
red and blue shovels
in the muddy spots
and lick
the chains of swings.

Everything reaches out
to everything else
yet time seems up and when
time is up runaways
can't get home, coastlines
fail, plans U-turn on blind
curves.

Dear Private Life,
Lived life is now
a home with no property,
street corner in a dream,
is a dream of off hours,

is a dream of a dream
of falling, failing to catch
a break that could lead
to transfiguration.

Sleeping and waking,
walking
and hobbling,
running with the memory
of skipping, sitting
with the memory
of the fallen;
time is loose
like sugar
spilled on a counter
it all cannot make it back
in the spoon.

And who is on the grass
where the single
blade is
ignored for
the whole
of it?

I will push ahead
let go a howl,
anyone listening will
get over it, some
might, like waves,
join in; more will act
as if they didn't
hear a thing.

One

The word
won't behave,
floats just
beyond me,
won't reveal
itself.

Aware of time
passing yet
I don't want to give
up.

Nothing helps me
so
a word that comes
close
is what I
swim to;

this takes up
time.

People don't understand,
pause,

not to mention,
silence.

I know there is
never
just one word,

all that exists
does
not rest
on just
one
word.

Jacqueline De Angelis is a poet and fiction writer who is the winner of the Crossing Boundaries Award for innovative and experimental writing, as well as, a finalist for the Emily Dickinson, Allen Ginsberg, and Finishing Line Press' New Women's Voices awards. Her poetry has been published in *Agni, International Quarterly, The Patterson Literary Review, Minute Magazine*, and in *Another City: Writing from Los Angeles*, City Lights Press, among other publications. She cofounded and published the first literary magazine and press started in Los Angeles by women: *rara avis/ Books of a Feather*. She received her MFA from Bennington College in Vermont and has taught writing workshops in various elementary, senior schools, and colleges. She has been in residency at Dorland Mountain Colony and Hedgebrook. She writes from Topanga Canyon in the Santa Monica Mountains and can be reached at http://www.jacquelinedeangelis.com

www.ingramcontent.com/pod-product-compliance
Lightning Source LLC
LaVergne TN
LVHW041506070426
835507LV00012B/1367